The Official Hibernian Football Club Annual 2009

Written By David Forsyth

A Grange Publication

© 2008. Published by Grange Communications Ltd., Edinburgh under licence from Hibernian Football Club. Printed in the EU.

Every effort has been made to ensure the accuracy of information within this publication but the publishers cannot be held responsible for any errors or omissions. Views expressed are those of the author and do not necessarily represent those of the publishers or the football club. All rights reserved.

ISBN 978-1-906211-35-6

Photographs © SNS Pix.
Special thanks to Tom Wright and Alan Rennie.

£6.99

CONTENTS

CONTENTS

Introduction 6
Chairman Welcome 8
Season Review 9
Player Quiz 22
New Signings 23
The Famous Five 24
The Manager 30
Mixu - The Player 32
New Signings 34
Nickname Quiz 35
Player Profiles 36
A Look At Our History 46
Profile - Ian Murray 48
Team Photo 50
Academy News 52
Ones to Watch 53
The Training Centre 56
Club Contacts 60
Quiz Answers 61

INTRODUCTION

INTRODUCTION

Welcome to the Official Hibernian 2009 Annual

Inside you will find profiles of the Squad, a chat with the Manager, a profile of the all-time Hibernian Greats, the Famous Five, a review of last season and a special feature on the Club's state of the art training centre.

We also take a look at Hibernian's famed Youth Academy, and readers can test their knowledge with our quizzes and brain teasers.

We hope you enjoy this year's edition and remember – Glory Glory to the Hibees!

CHAIRMAN'S WELCOME

Each season brings its own challenges, its own highs and its own lows, and season 07/08 proved to be something of a rollercoaster.

We enjoyed a thrilling start to the season in which the Club enjoyed the longest unbeaten run in the SPL; we then saw a slump in form with a long period in which points proved hard to come by, and the team dropped down the league.

Then came the high of finally opening our new, state-of-the-art training centre in East Lothian, a match for anything in the country and a major investment in the Football Club at around £5 million.

Sadly, this was to be followed all too quickly by another low, this time the shock resignation of then Manager John Collins.

However, following an exhaustive search for a successor, the Board appointed former player Mixu Paatelainen, who immediately set about tackling the form slump and – after bringing in several new players – the team forced their way back up the league table and were strongly in contention for a coveted UEFA Cup slot until the final two or three matches.

Mixu is, of course, a great favourite at Easter Road, having enjoyed two spells with the Club as a player, and his enthusiasm and appetite for the task in hand bode well for the Club's future.

In a wider context, Scottish fans enjoyed the resurgence of the national team, who narrowly failed to qualify for Euro 2008 from the toughest of groups, while the demise of Gretna

ROD PETRIE, CHAIRMAN

demonstrated the continued need for clubs to live within their means.

As ever, the Board will do all that it can to ensure we give the Manager every support to meet his own aspirations, those of the Board and – most important – those of the loyal and valued supporters, whilst taking care that the Club continues to be run in a sustainable way to ensure that our children and grandchildren can enjoy watching and supporting Hibernian.

SEASON REVIEW

JULY
Pre-season saw the team based in Austria, where a warm-up game was lost against local opposition before the squad headed back to begin competitive friendlies back in Scotland, chalking up wins against Brechin, Stirling Albion and Livingston before earning two home wins against Premiership opposition, seeing off both Bolton and Middlesbrough without conceding a goal. ▶

SEASON REVIEW

SEASON REVIEW

AUGUST

The SPL season kicked off in the most dramatic fashion possible, with an away tie at Tynecastle against arch-rivals Hearts. Hibernian fans were to enjoy the day, with new boy Brian Kerr slotting home the only goal of the game in a match which was more comfortable than the scoreline suggested. Gretna were despatched at Easter Road next, after going 2-0 in front. A shock was avoided following a Zemmama-inspired fightback which saw Hibs score four times. A difficult away trip to Tannadice to face a resurgent Dundee United ended in a 0-0 draw, and another home fightback, this time against Aberdeen, saw a 3-3 scoreline with Zemmama, Fletcher and Shiels all scoring. The month ended with the team beginning their defence of the CIS Cup, winning 2-1 away to Queen's Park at Hampden. ▶

SEASON REVIEW

NOVEMBER

Hearts were first to come calling at Easter Road in November, and another hard-fought derby ended with honours shared 1-1, with the Hibs score coming courtesy of an own goal. Gretna, playing at their "home from home" at Motherwell, provided the opposition for the next match and put up stout resistance before going down 1-0 to the Hibees with Fletcher netting. The final match of the month saw Dundee United visit, and a thrilling encounter again saw these two share the points in a 2-2 draw with Benjelloun and Antoine-Curier the scorers for Hibs.

SEASON REVIEW

DECEMBER

A busy December, as ever, kicked off at Pittodrie with a 3-1 defeat, with Fletcher scoring Hibs' only goal. The match was to kick off a disappointing slump in form. Another long trek away, this time to Inverness, ended in further disappointment and a 2-0 defeat. Falkirk came calling at Easter Road, and a Clayton Donaldson penalty earned Hibs a 1-1 draw in what was to prove John Collins' final match in charge. The manager shocked Hibernian fans with his unexpected resignation just a couple of days before the team travelled to Parkhead under the charge of caretaker manager Tommy Craig. A fine performance saw David Murphy score in a 1-1 draw at the home of the champions. Dean Shiels scored from the spot the following match, away to Kilmarnock, in a 2-1 defeat and the month ended with another loss, this time 2-1 to Rangers at Easter Road with Zemmama netting a late consolation.

SEASON REVIEW

SEASON REVIEW

JANUARY

An away trip to St Mirren was to prove Tommy Craig's final match in charge, as the team went down 2-1 with Antoine-Curier the scorer. New manager Mixu Paatelainen was in the dug-out with his assistant, Donald Park, for the visit of Inverness in a Scottish Cup tie at Easter Road. The team played high tempo, exciting football with Dean Shiels the star of the show with a hat-trick and a man-of-the-match performance in a 3-0 win. The third round of SPL fixtures kicked off with a return visit to Tynecastle, and this time Hibernian were unlucky to go down by the only goal. A number of new faces arrived, including John Rankin from Inverness, Colin Nish from Kilmarnock, Martin Canning as a free agent, Aberraouf Zarabi from French football and one Ian Murray from Norwich. ▶

SEASON REVIEW

FEBRUARY

Rangers were first up in the 5th Round of the Scottish Cup at Easter Road. Despite dominating the match, the game ended 0-0 and a replay was arranged for Ibrox. A trip to Dundee United on league business again ended, for the third meeting between the sides, in a draw – this time 1-1 – showing yet again how little there was between the two teams. Gretna were the visitors in the following game, and were comfortably beaten 4-2 with Fletcher scoring a hat-trick and January signing Colin Nish getting off the mark. The team continued in its winning ways with a 3-1 home demolition of Aberdeen, the goals coming from Fletcher, Shiels and Zemmama, and another home win followed, with Inverness beaten 2-0 with goals from Nish and Fletcher. An away trip to Falkirk concluded the month, with John Rankin and an own goal contributing to the 2-0 win.

SEASON REVIEW

PLAYER QUIZ ANSWERS ON P61

1. From which Club did Colin Nish sign in January 08?

2. Mixu Paatelainen was capped for which country?

3. Which country does Dean Shiels represent?

4. Which Hibernian player scored for Partick Thistle in a cup tie last season?

5. Name the two players who kept goal for Hibernian last season?

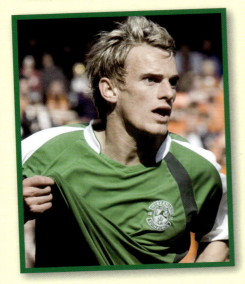

6. Which Spanish giant did Hibernian face in a pre-season friendly this year?

LATE NEWS

Two exciting new players were added to the Hibernian squad in August 2008.

Fabian Yantorno, the Uruguayan star well-known to Scottish fans due to his appearances for Gretna, signed a two year deal with the Club.

The attacking midfielder spent several months at the Club's East Lothian training centre, undergoing rehabilitation from a serious knee injury, before proving his fitness and earning his new deal.

Fabian (26) had been left without assistance after Gretna went into administration, before Manager Mixu Paatelainen stepped in to offer the midfielder training and treatment at East Lothian.

He was joined on the squad list by Steve Pinau, who joined the Club on a one-year loan deal from Serie A side Genoa.

Striker Steve, who is a French under-19 international, came through the ranks at AS Monaco before earning a move to Italy. He is 20 years old.

The Manager said: "These are two exciting and talented players who will get the fans out of their seats, so I am delighted we have them both. It improves competition and that should help us achieve greater consistency."

THE FAMOUS FIVE

Hibernian has a rich history, in which a number of firsts have been achieved, but the number Five is one that bears greatest significance for a huge number of followers of the Club and its history.

The Famous Five is arguably the greatest forward line ever to grace the Scottish game, and the players who made up that attack all remain legends – Gordon Smith, Bobby Johnstone, Lawrie Reilly, Eddie Turnbull and Willie Ormond.

Undoubtedly the Five and their team-mates gave the Club the richest period in its history. No group of players to wear the famous green-and-white shirts have ever achieved more. Back to back league titles in seasons 1950-51 and 51-52 were their greatest achievement, but there were numerous others.

April 14th 1949 was the day the Five first played together, in a friendly between Hibernian and Nithsdale Wanderers at Sanquhar in south-west Scotland. The first competitive match came on October 15th at Easter Road. The promotion of Bobby Johnstone from the reserves brought the Five together in a league encounter against Queen of the South, with Turnbull and Smith finding the net in a 2-0 win.

Only three games were lost that season, and the club finished runners-up to Rangers.

The following year, all that changed. Hibs reached the League Cup Final, the Scottish Cup Semi-Final and won the league – with Lawrie Reilly banging in 23 goals to top the club scoring charts.

The Club defended the league title the following season, Reilly bagging 27 goals to see Hibernian beat Rangers by four clear points and scoring 96 goals in their 30 matches.

The following season the team was pipped by the narrowest of margins on goal average by Rangers. Had the more modern goal difference applied, Hibernian would again have been crowned league champions. In total, 92 goals were scored by the free-wheeling attack, with Reilly scoring no fewer than six hat-tricks.

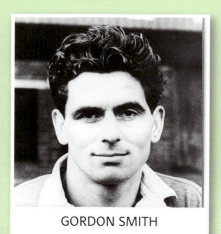

GORDON SMITH

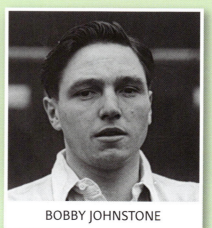

BOBBY JOHNSTONE

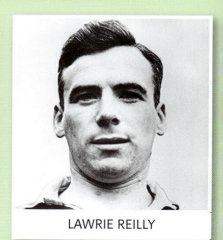

LAWRIE REILLY

Many observers felt that all of the Five should have been chosen together to represent Scotland, but that never happened. Four was the greatest number picked to play together in the dark blue at any one time.

The final match in which the Famous Five played together was on January 29th, 1955 against Clyde, which was lost 2-3. In March that year the Five was split up when Bobby Johnstone was transferred to Manchester City for the then substantial sum of £22,000.

The Five enjoyed a glorious international history as well as domestically.

Then chairman Harry Swan and manager Willie McCartney had the vision to believe that foreign tours and travel would help the Club develop, and in 1953 Hibernian were invited to play in a tournament in Brazil, gracing the world

"We toured the world, and while we learned a lot on our travels I would like to think that others learned from us as well." REILLY

EDDIE TURNBULL

WILLIE ORMOND

NEW SIGNINGS

Two players who can bolster the midfield area were signed earlier this year.

Joe Keenan signed a two-year deal with the Club this summer. A 26-year-old midfielder born in Southampton, Joe started his career at Chelsea as a trainee, making two appearances for the Premiership side, his first coming in 2002, before a leg break sustained in a Chelsea reserve game against London rivals Arsenal forced him out for an extended spell. He made 4 appearances in England for Brentford. More recently however Joe has had a spell in Australia with Melbourne Victory.

Steven Thicot signed a three-year deal. Steven is a 21-year-old defender and midfielder who started his career in France at INF Clairefontaine before joining Nantes in 2002. He had a spell at CS Sedan-Ardennes in 2006 before rejoining Nantes last season. Steven was a member of the French Under-17 European Championship winning side in 2004.

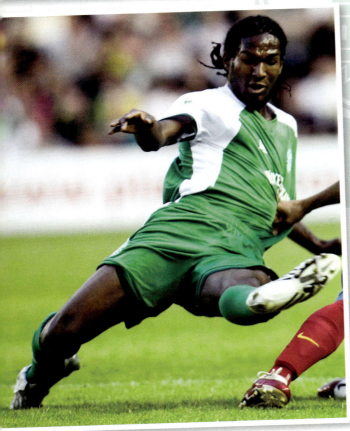

Signing the players, Mixu Paatelainen said: "Both players will prove to be excellent additions to our squad. Joe has done very well since coming to us on trial and has impressed both in training and in games. Steven is a young player who shows a great deal of maturity and a fantastic approach to the game. He is a very good player who can play in a number of positions and has come through all the French national teams alongside some of the top players in the world. He has plenty of ability and like Joe is a very ambitious footballer, which is something I like to see."

NICKNAME QUIZ
ANSWERS ON P61

1. Who was known as "The Quiet Man?"

2. Which Hibernian star was nicknamed "Le God" by supporters?

3. Which one of the Famous Five was known as "The Prince of Wingers?"

4. Easter Road is sometimes called after a world-famous Italian ground, which will complete the phrase "the Leith…?"

5. A League Cup winning star was known simply as "Keef". Can you name him?

6. The successful Hibernian team of the early 70s was named after its manager as …?

7. Which Hibernian keeper went on to become known as "The Goalie?"

8. Which manager of Hibernian was known as "Mogga?"

PLAYER PROFILES

GOALKEEPERS

Andy McNeil

Andy McNeil enjoyed a stunning end to last season after coming into the team due to an injury to Yves Ma-Kalambay. A series of top drawer displays, including a number of world-class saves – in particular against Falkirk and St Mirren - saw him beat off the tough competition of the big Belgian to keep the jersey until the season finished. Andy (21) joined Hibernian from Southampton in January 2006 and he was delighted to come to Easter Road after growing up as a fan of the Club.

Yves Ma-Kalambay

Yves Ma-Kalambay enjoyed a successful first season between the sticks at Hibernian after joining the Club in summer 2007 from Chelsea. The 22-year-old giant – who stands 6ft 6ins tall – played a total of 33 matches before an injury gave team-mate Andy McNeil a chance to stake his claim. Powerful, commanding and agile, Yves is a popular figure with fans.

David Grof

Not too many players can claim to have made their debut against the star-studded Barcelona, but that is precisely the claim David Grof can make. The Hungarian teenager came on with around ten minutes remaining of Hibernian's pre-season friendly against the Catalan giants. Shortly afterwards, David faced English Premiership opposition, when the club played Wigan in a pre-season friendly. The imposing youngster stands well over six feet tall, and his greatest attributes are his agility and his confidence. David will be hoping that this season sees him challenge for a more regular slot in the first team squads.

PLAYER PROFILES
DEFENDERS

Rob Jones

Rob Jones is a tower of strength at the heart of the Hibernian defence. The 6ft 7in centre back came to the Club in the summer of 2006 in a £100,000 move from English Championship side Grimsby. As well as his defensive qualities, Rob always provides a threat for opposition sides from set pieces. While he failed to match the goalscoring exploits of his first season in Scotland, tight marking on the big centre half leaves room for others to exploit.

Chris Hogg

Chris Hogg is Hibernian's Mr Consistency, and last season was most pundits' pick as our player of the year. After an injury-blighted start to his career at Easter Road, Chris (23) has matured into one of the team's natural leaders. The former England youth captain joined the Club from Ipswich Town and has pace, courage, timing in the tackle and aerial ability.

PLAYER PROFILES
DEFENDERS

Kevin McCann

Kevin McCann made his breakthrough in season 2006/07, but his progress last season was largely hampered by injury. The 21-year-old, a product of the Hibernian youth system, continues to show maturity beyond his years at right-back and will be hoping this season sees him stay clear of niggling injuries.

David Van Zanten

David Van Zanten joined Hibernian on a pre-contract at the end of last season, signing a three-year deal at Easter Road. David, who has a Dutch father and an Irish mother, joined the Club from SPL side St Mirren, where he had played for five years, being an integral part of the Paisley side that gained promotion to the SPL in season 2005-06. He joined Celtic in 1999 as a teenager, and spent three seasons at Parkhead. Manager Mixu Paatelainen was keen to recruit a player he knew well from his own time at St Mirren as a player/coach. He said: "He is a talented professional who can play in a number of positions. I am delighted we got him."

PLAYER PROFILES

Darren McCormack

Darren McCormack has made just six appearances to date for the first team, but the tough, uncompromising style of his play has already won him many fans. The youngster can play at either full back or centre back, and looks to be a real talent for the future.

Martin Canning

Martin Canning joined the Club as a free agent last season, after buying himself out of his contract with Gretna. The powerful centre-back made ten appearances for the first team, and slotted in at both centre-back and, on occasions, at full-back. A calm and assured presence.

Paul Hanlon

Paul Hanlon is the latest recruit from the Hibernian Youth Academy to break through into the first team, slotting in as an 18-year-old right back and earning high praise for polished displays. A tall, imposing player, he can also play at centre back.

PLAYER PROFILES
DEFENDER/MIDFIELDERS

Lewis Stevenson

Lewis Stevenson is yet another product of the Hibernian Academy, and the 20-year-old is a flexible left-sided player. Again, injury hampered his development after an outstanding season in 2006/07, but the young man who is equally at home in midfield or at left-back has much to look forward to.

Ian Murray

Ian Murray returned to the Club where he developed as a player in January this year, moving from Norwich. Mr Versatility, he has performed to a high standard at left back, right back, centre back and in midfield. The former club captain provides athleticism, a winning mentality, commitment and drive.

PLAYER PROFILES

MIDFIELDERS

Merouane Zemmama

Merouane Zemmama – or Zouma - is a player who gets fans out of their seats with his close control, pace and searing shot. The Moroccan joined the Club from Raja Casablanca and he is a box of attacking tricks who has a key role to play at the Club. The 25-year-old playmaker has made 57 appearances for the Club.

Dean Shiels

Dean Shiels is another talented and clever footballer. He joined Hibernian after coming through the famous Arsenal Academy. An intelligent and hard-working player, he fought back from eye surgery and his whole-hearted style coupled with his ability to score vital goals has won many admirers for the 23-year-old.

PLAYER PROFILES
MIDFIELDERS

Ross Chisholm

Ross Chisholm continued to progress last season, and much will be expected of him this year. He is another product of the Hibernian Academy and as a central midfielder has impressed the manager with some mature displays and his ability to play box to box, tackling and passing.

Alan O'Brien

Alan O'Brien (23) is a lightning-quick attacking midfielder who joined the Club in the summer of 2007 from Newcastle United. The Republic of Ireland international made a total of 29 appearances, most of those from the bench, and he will be looking to play a greater role this season.

PLAYER PROFILES

Filipe Morais

Filipe Morais (23) is a tricky wide player, who joined the Club last season from Millwall. A Portugese U-21 international, he turned professional with Chelsea and his jinking style and powerful shot have seen him score two goals in his 32 appearances to date.

John Rankin

John Rankin was brought to the Club by Mixu Paatelainen from Inverness Caledonian Thistle. The left-sided midfielder has earned much praise for his all-action style, and he weighed in with two goals from his 19 appearances.

PLAYER PROFILES
STRIKERS

Steven Fletcher

Steven Fletcher had a fine season, finishing as the Club's top scorer. Highlight for the 21-year-old was making his full international debut, and he looks certain to play a key role at that level for many years to come. A talented and lethal left foot, tremendous work-rate, pace, mobility and courage are all hallmarks of his play.

Damon Gray

Damon Gray has been enjoying a period on loan at First Division Partick Thistle following a productive spell with The Jags last season, including scoring a memorable Scottish Cup goal for the Jags against Rangers at Ibrox. A natural finisher, the Geordie-born striker will look to continue to progress.

PLAYER PROFILES

Ross Campbell

Ross Campbell finished the season well, the youngster forcing his way into the first team squad to bring his Hibernian career appearances to 10. The 21 year-old allies his workrate with being quick, clever and a natural finisher.

Colin Nish

Colin Nish joined Hibernian in January from Kilmarnock. The striker, a Hibs fan, quickly became a hit with supporters through forging a productive and entertaining strike partnership with Steven Fletcher. Nish scored 4 times in 15 appearances, and the tall hitman will look to build on that return this season.

PROFILE – IAN MURRAY

It had the feeling of a homecoming when Mr Versatility Ian Murray returned to Easter Road in January 2008.

The defender/midfielder was one of manager Mixu Paatelainen's first signings – based on the Manager's first-hand knowledge of Ian as a player and a team-mate.

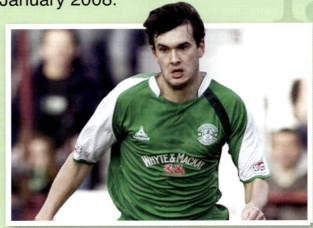

And while "Nidd's" departure for Rangers in the summer of 2005 rankled with sections of the Easter Road support, all was swiftly forgotten as Ian turned in his usual string of totally committed performances – a point he was quick to acknowledge.

And he insisted he returned to Easter Road a better player after his illness-hit spell at Rangers and a short time at Norwich City. "I think I am a better, more mature player now and that the experiences I have gained will stand me in good stead.

"I think supporters also recognise that I am glad to be back at Hibs, and that I will give 100% at all times – as I always have done."

The player once described by former Manager Alex McLeish as "having the heart of a lion" has again demonstrated his ability to play to a high level across a number of positions, appearing in both full-back roles, at centre-half and in midfield. The debate never leaves him:

"I like to play centre-half or central midfield but I suppose it's that old cliché, I'll play anywhere if it means I get a game. The manager knows what I like and while he might ask me to play full-back for a few games he knows where I prefer longer term."

The Manager believes Ian is best suited as a midfield player "because of his engine" but added that his strong defensive abilities meant that he was perhaps most effective as a defensive midfielder.

Mixu was also keen to stress the reasons he was keen to bring Ian home to Easter Road: "He is still quite young but he is very experienced. He has played at international level and at a high level in European competition. He has tremendous commitment and is a brave player who doesn't hide when the going gets tough."

First game back for Ian was, fittingly for the Hibs-daft player, an Edinburgh derby at Tynecastle which Hibernian narrowly lost 1-0. However Ian's own performance was highly praised by fans and by pundits.

He said: "It was probably the best possible game for me to come back into. I love playing in these games.

"The response of the supporters to me was terrific."

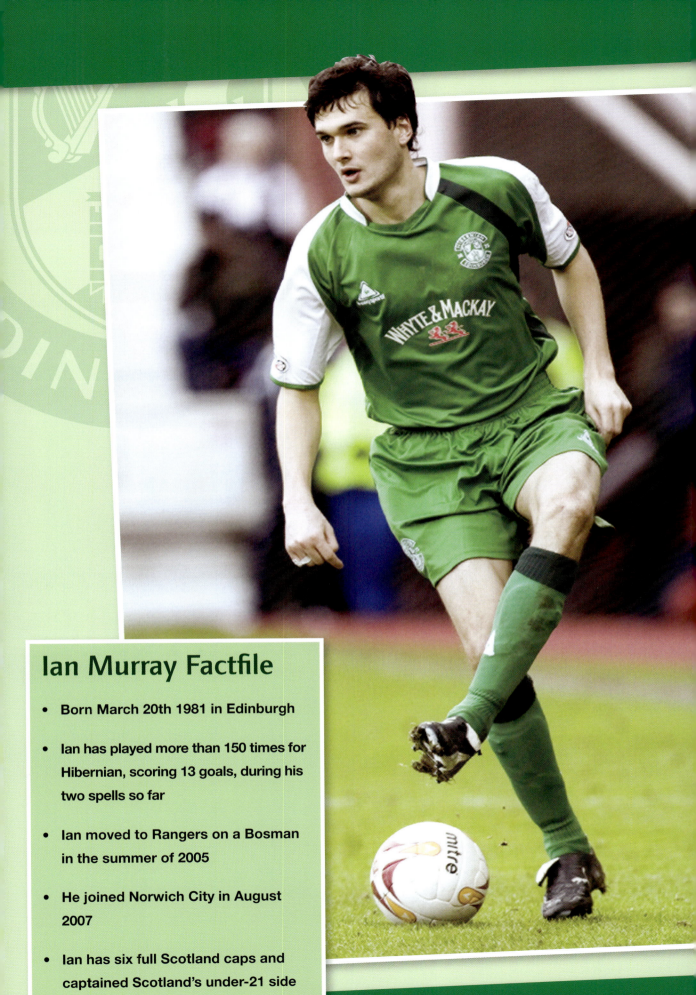

Ian Murray Factfile

- Born March 20th 1981 in Edinburgh

- Ian has played more than 150 times for Hibernian, scoring 13 goals, during his two spells so far

- Ian moved to Rangers on a Bosman in the summer of 2005

- He joined Norwich City in August 2007

- Ian has six full Scotland caps and captained Scotland's under-21 side

HIBERNIAN F.C.

THE TEAM

ACADEMY NEWS

ONES TO WATCH

Ross Campbell, striker

Scotland under-21 internationalist Ross Campbell is a quick, mobile striker with an eye for goal.

Ross first broke into the first team in competitive matches near the start of 2007, when the team was under the stewardship of John Collins.

His appearances have been restricted by the outstanding form of more experienced players, in particular Steven Fletcher and Colin Nish, but a run of matches towards the end of last season must have given the 21-year-old the belief that season 2008/09 could be his big year.

Ross has represented his country at a number of levels, most notably during the 2007 under-20 World Cup in Canada where he scored in a match against Japan.

Callum Booth, defender

Callum has been in the Hibernian Academy since the age of 11 and has been a registered player for the Club since 2002.

He took up a regular left back slot in the under-19s team halfway through last season following the promotion of Paul Hanlon to the first team.

Callum lives close to the training centre in East Lothian – which makes a welcome change for him. Over the years Callum has travelled further than most boys in the system, as for a number of years, he made a weekly journey to the Academy training venue in Motherwell.

Turning professional has seen Callum make excellent progress and, in addition to his defensive duties as a left back, he carries a potent attacking threat with his surging runs down the left flank. He also has an eye for goal, and in the preseason matches this year scored 3 goals.

THE TRAINING CENTRE

It was a proud day for all associated with Hibernian when the Club opened its top class new training centre a year ago.

The centre, which is as good as any in Scotland and more than a match for the facilities enjoyed by most English Premiership sides, was officially opened by the Club's majority shareholder, Sir Tom Farmer CBE KCSG DL.

The centre includes five international-sized grass pitches, and one international sized and fully floodlit synthetic surface which meets the highest Fifa requirements. There is also an indoor short-sided artificial surface, while inside the facilities include a large, fully equipped gym, extensive changing rooms, medical rooms, a hydro-therapy suite, players' lounge, coaches' room, dining rooms, offices and meeting rooms.

There are also complementary facilities, such as video editing to assist with match analysis.

Manager Mixu Paatelainen said: "The Training Centre is just fantastic, and provides the highest quality environment for our players to work together, to train and to develop as footballers. It will help the Club's development for many years to come."

CLUB CONTACTS

CLUB ADDRESS

HIBERNIAN FOOTBALL CLUB
Easter Road Stadium
12 Albion Place
Edinburgh
EH7 5QG
Tel: 0131 661 2159
Ticket Box Office: 0131 661 1875

MATCH-DAY HOSPITALITY & ADVERTISING

AMANDA VETTESE,
Corporate Hospitality Manager
avettese@hibernianfc.co.uk
Tel: 0131 656 7073

ANNA DEVINE
Commerical Manager
adevine@hibernianfc.co.uk
Tel: 0131 656 7072

GENERAL ENQUIRIES

club@hibernianfc.co.uk
Tel: 0131 661 2159

CLUB STORE

RICHARD ALEXANDER
Manager, Retail Operations
ralexander@hibernianfc.co.uk
Store - Tel: 0131 656 7078 / 0131 656 7097

TICKET OPERATIONS

JUDITH IRELAND
Ticket Office Manager
jquinn@hibernianfc.co.uk
Tel: 0131 661 1875 / 0844 844 1875 (Option 2)

CONFERENCE & BANQUETING

All Enquiries to:
Tel: 0131 656 7075

QUIZ ANSWERS

Quiz Answers

PLAYER QUIZ P22

1. Kilmarnock 2. Finland 3. Northern Ireland 4. Damon Gray
5. Andy McNeil + Yves Ma-Kalambay 6. Barcelona

NICKNAMES QUIZ P35

1. Pat Stanton 2. Frank Sauzee 3. Gordon Smith
4. San Siro 5. Keith Wright 6. Turnbull's Tornadoes
7. Andy Goram 8. Tony Mowbray